ZooBreak
ANIMALS ON THE RUN

Contents

Steck Vaughn™

A Harcourt Achieve Imprint

www.Steck-Vaughn.com
1-800-531-5015

Hi, I'm Zookeeper Lisa. I'll be your guide in this book. As you know, most animals don't speak English. Don't worry! I've translated everything so that you can follow along.

But first, here are a couple of things you'll want to keep in mind.

Big Ideas

- Animals are born with certain behaviors already programmed into their brains. These behaviors are called instincts. Animals don't need to learn them.

- The ability to learn is important for the survival of every animal.

- Animals use many different types of learning. Some things are learned through practice. Some are learned by watching others.

- Animals use many forms of communication. Some use sounds to convey meanings similar to the way humans do.

Do animals think like you and me? Wait until you see these chimps try to escape. They'll use all of their intelligence. Plus, they'll get some help from their friends.

Before you read further, check out the words below. They will help you track those chimps.

Vocabulary

intelligence the ability to think, learn, and understand
The student's intelligence showed that she knew the science material.

observe to watch something or someone carefully
I observed the large dog in my front yard.

predator an animal that hunts other animals for food
The lion is a predator who hunts zebra and antelope.

predict to say what will happen in the future
Because of all the clouds, I predict it will rain tomorrow.

prey an animal that is hunted by other animals for food
The tiger's prey ran up the tree.

Characters

Niki,
chimpanzee

Max,
chimpanzee

Jak,
Max's brother

Polly,
wasp

Melissa,
honey bee

Lola,
squid

Squeak,
meerkat

Squeal,
meerkat

Tangle,
raven

Lisa,
Zookeeper

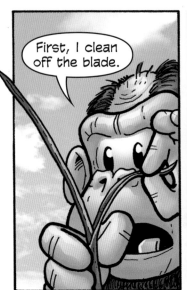

First, I clean off the blade.

Next, I lick the grass to make it sticky.

Then, I stick it into the ant mound.

And finally, I pull out a snack Just like mom showed me!

Cultural learning happens by watching someone else do something. Chimps learn to use tools by watching their parents.

What are you doing now?

I'm replacing the grass.

Why do you worry about lower animals? They're completely different from us.

Let me show you something.

This circle represents us. We are *mammals*. We each have four limbs, hair, and a brain.

This circle is Polly. She is an insect. She has six limbs, no hair, and a brain.

See, we both have brains! We both think.

Can wasps make tools like us?

No. But, you should *observe* them. Look at the complex nests they build. There are different kinds of *intelligence*.

7

8

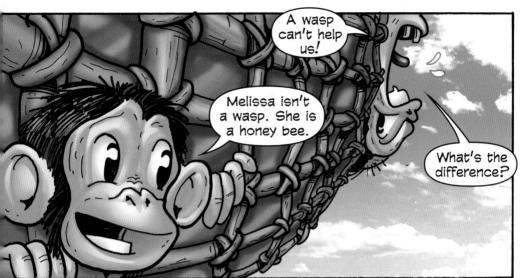

A wasp can't help us!

Melissa isn't a wasp. She is a honey bee.

What's the difference?

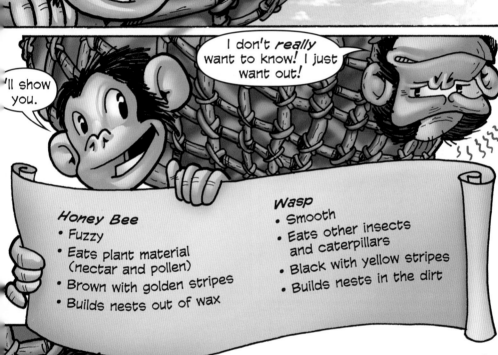

I'll show you.

I don't *really* want to know! I just want out!

Honey Bee
- Fuzzy
- Eats plant material (nectar and pollen)
- Brown with golden stripes
- Builds nests out of wax

Wasp
- Smooth
- Eats other insects and caterpillars
- Black with yellow stripes
- Builds nests in the dirt

See, honey bees and wasps are quite different. Bees can even tell other bees where flowers are. Wasps can't do that.

Hi, Max.

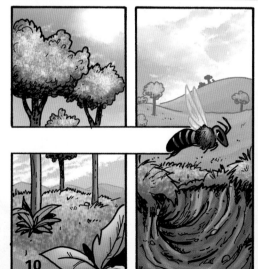

Honey bees communicate using **symbolic logic**. A symbol is something that stands for something else. For example, a green traffic light means "go." The waggle dance is all about distance and direction.

Are you okay?

We're fine.

I'm fine. Super Chimp is having a panic attack.

WE ARE NOT FINE!

What can we do?

Hi, Squeak and Squeal. Please stand guard for us.

What good are those tiny guards?

Meerkats have over 900 different alarm calls. They can signal danger for everything from snakes to jackals.

That's symbolic logic again!

They can warn us before a *predator* sneaks up and eats us.

What are you two looking at? *Get to work!*

12

Insight learning means taking what you already learned and using it to solve a new problem.

13

15

Conditioning is making a connection between a **stimulus** or signal and a **reward** or **punishment**. It's like when you feel hungry from watching a pizza commercial. The commercial is the stimulus.

16

These screw-top lids are easy to open.

Thank you, Lola!

GRAB MEAT

BIRDHOUSE →
← SQUID

BIRDHOUSE EMPLOYEES ONLY

Hey, Tangle, I need your help.

I'm sleeping.

What's taking so long?

Please be patient. This requires a certain amount of trial and error.

I got it.

ZIP Crash!

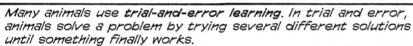

Many animals use **trial-and-error learning**. In trial and error, animals solve a problem by trying several different solutions until something finally works.

Good work, Tangle. Let's go get those ants.

I'm free!

You should thank these "lower" animals.

Okay. You've made your point.

Excuse us, but we have a problem.

What is it now? A hippo? Where's your alarm call?

That's the problem.

We have no alarm call for wasps.

19

Wrap Up

Niki and Max finally escaped from the net. A lot of their friends helped, too. Of course, chimps don't really talk to other kinds of animals, but you get the point! All creatures have their own type of intelligence.

All animals use certain innate skills called instincts. They are born with these. Some animals use skills that they learn from trial and error. Some skills are learned from watching other animals.

I know some real-life animals that can do amazing things. One gorilla named Koko can speak sign language! Alex the parrot can count objects. And all ruby-throated hummingbirds can find their way home alone—across the Gulf of Mexico! Now that takes brains!

To find how smart animals really are, take a look at *Animal Smarts: What Do They Really Know?*

ANIMAL SMARTS
What Do They Really Know?

Debra Hess

Glossary

condition (*verb*) to train someone to do something or to behave in a certain way

cultural learning (*noun*) learning that happens by watching someone else do something

doomed (*adjective*) certain to suffer a terrible fate

insight learning (*noun*) learning that happens by using what you have already learned to solve a new problem

instinct (*noun*) behavior that a person or animal is born with and does not have to learn

intelligence (*noun*) the ability to think, learn, and understand

mammal (*noun*) a warm-blooded animal that has a back bone

observe (*verb*) to watch something or someone carefully

predator (*noun*) an animal that hunts other animals for food

predict (*verb*) to say what will happen in the future

prey (*noun*) an animal that is hunted by other animals for food

raven (*noun*) a large, crow-like bird that has shiny black feathers and a harsh cry

spatial learning (*noun*) learning that happens by memorizing where objects are in someone's environment

stimulus (*noun*) something that causes an action

symbolic logic (*noun*) the use of symbols to communicate

trial-and-error learning (*noun*) learning that happens by trying several different solutions to a problem

Idioms

you can say that again (*page 10*) to agree very strongly with something someone said
It's a long time until lunch? You can say that again.

it's a deal (*page 16*) to come to an agreement
If you'll sell the computer at that price, then it's a deal!